Imagination.

FACT or CRaP

It's your call!

Test yourself & friends
with bizarre trivia!

Published and distributed by Imagination,
6161 Santa Monica Boulevard, Suite 100, Los Angeles
CA 90038, USA; Suite 1.14 Network House,
Bradfield Close, Woking GU22 7RE, UK and
64 North Terrace, Kent Town SA 5067, Australia.
www.imaginationgames.com

First Printing 2007
5 4 3 2 1

Printed in Canada

ISBN(10) – 1-934524-03-4
ISBN(13) – 978-1-934524-03-9

We would be happy to hear your questions or
comments about this book. Write to: Imagination,
Consumer Advice Department, 64 North Terrace,
Kent Town, South Australia, 5067, Australia
or email contactus@imaginationgames.com

Contents

Introduction

Get ready to play the fun-filled trivia game that only has two answers – Fact or Crap! It's designed to test your wit, your skill and your knowledge of just about everything, from the day to day, to the truly bizarre.

Based on the hit board game of the same name, you can play by yourself ... or challenge your friends, anywhere, anytime.

With 20 individual games and 600 all-new questions, your aim is to dazzle your opposition, or yourself, with just how much you know (or don't know) about the world.

Earn bonus points for getting all questions correct ... and watch out for the madcap Rush Hour rounds, where you'll score double ... or nothing. It's fast, it's fun, and it's full of fascinating facts – you just need to pick out the crap! With the Hall of Fame, or Shame, awaiting your name, you could be immortalized or mortified.

It's your call, but remember, it comes down to two words: Fact or Crap. Good luck!

How to play

The Fact or Crap Quiz Book contains 20 individual games, each with 3 rounds of questions ... two standard and one Rush Hour round. If you don't want to mark your book, have spare paper handy to mark down your answers or use the notes section at the back of the book.

Multi Player Game
All players divide into two teams, A and B. Team B reads out Team A's questions and vice versa. Team members can take turns answering, or collaborate before giving their answer. Answers can be written down on a piece of paper, or the opposition can note them in the book.

Check the answers at the end of each round. You'll find them upside down at the bottom of each page. At the end of the game, add up your scores to see who is better at picking the Fact from the Crap.

Single Player Game
If you are playing solo, work your way through both teams' questions and mark your answers for each round, then total your game score. If you think you deserve it, put your name into the Hall of Fame. The good thing about playing alone is that no one's going to outscore you.

How to play (continued)

Rounds 1 & 2

In these standard rounds, each correct answer is worth 1 point. If you get all five answers right, you also score 2 bonus points.

Rush Hour Round

Answer all questions correctly and you score 10 big points ... BUT ... get just one answer wrong and you score zilch.

For a little extra zip, why not add a time limit to the Rush Hour Round.

Scoring

The team with the highest score wins not only the game, but the chance to have their name and score immortalized in the Hall of Fame. Unfortunately for the losing team, the dreaded Hall of Shame awaits.

Enjoy!

Game One

Here we go with Game 1. Team B, you read the questions to Team A first. Check the answers on the bottom of the page at the end of each round. Remember, there really are only two answers to choose from – Fact or Crap. Good luck!

Team A - Round 1

Team B, get ready to ask Team A these five questions. Every correct answer is worth one point. Get all five right and score a bonus 2 points.

1	Chevy Chase was the original anchor on Saturday Night Live's *Weekend Update*.	**FACT** CRaP
2	A parapet is an architectural style used in castles.	**FACT** CRaP
3	The Gregorian calendar does not factor in leap years.	**FACT** CRaP
4	Montezuma is best known for his leadership role among the Iroquois.	**FACT** CRaP
5	The Patriot Act never actually passed in Congress.	**FACT** CRaP

FACT for correct answer, **CRaP** for incorrect answer.

SCORE:

Team B - Round 1

Team A, get ready to ask Team B these five questions. Every correct answer is worth one point. Get all five right and score a bonus 2 points.

1	The Salem witch trials began in 1692.	**FACT** CRaP
2	Arnold Schwarzenegger was actually born in Paris.	**FACT** CRaP
3	Stubbing your toe is considered bad luck in Malawi.	**FACT** CRaP
4	Cassandra is the name of B.B. King's famous guitar.	**FACT** CRaP
5	*Happy Birthday* was the first song performed *in outer* space.	**FACT** CRaP

(**FACT**) for correct answer, (CRaP) for incorrect answer.

SCORE:

ANSWERS: 1) FACT 2) CRAP 3) CRAP 4) CRAP 5) FACT

Team A - Round 2

Team B, get ready to ask Team A these five questions. Every correct answer is worth one point. Get all five right and score a bonus 2 points.

1	Lincoln is the capital of South Dakota.	**FACT** CRaP
2	MTV's *Real World* reality TV series launched in 1992 in New York.	**FACT** CRaP
3	One large egg contains 16 grams of protein.	**FACT** CRaP
4	Nixon had a presidential pooch named Timahoe.	**FACT** CRaP
5	Jack Kerouac's net worth was less than $100 when he died.	**FACT** CRaP

FACT for correct answer, **CRaP** for incorrect answer.

SCORE:

Team B - Round 2

Team A, get ready to ask Team B these five questions. Every correct answer is worth one point. Get all five right and score a bonus 2 points.

1	Run DMC was the first rap group to perform on American Bandstand.	**FACT** CRaP
2	Olivia Newton-John had to be sewn into her pants in the final scene of *Grease*.	**FACT** CRaP
3	Bob Dylan broke his neck in a motorcycle crash.	**FACT** CRaP
4	The Art of Noise's cover recording of *Kiss* sold more than the original Prince version.	**FACT** CRaP
5	The tank top Bruce Willis wore in *Die Hard* is now in the Smithsonian Institute.	**FACT** CRaP

FACT for correct answer, CRaP for incorrect answer.

SCORE:

Team A - Rush Hour

Team B, get ready to call out the questions. Answer all questions correctly for 10 points, but get just one wrong and you score zilch.

1	Impeachment can only occur at the federal level of US government.	**FACT** CRaP
2	Michelangelo's *David* took 17 years to complete.	**FACT** CRaP
3	President Grant is not buried in Grant's tomb.	**FACT** CRaP
4	Afghanistan held its first democratic election on January 30, 2005.	**FACT** CRaP
5	The Coliseum in Rome predates England's Stonehenge.	**FACT** CRaP

(FACT) for correct answer, (CRaP) for incorrect answer.

SCORE:

ANSWERS: 1) CRAP 2) CRAP 3) FACT 4) CRAP 5) CRAP

Team B - Rush Hour

Team A, get ready to call out the questions. Answer all questions correctly for 10 points, but get just one wrong and you score zilch.

1	The first NFL game was televised in October 1939.	**FACT** CRaP
2	There are 1665 stairs leading up the Eiffel Tower.	**FACT** CRaP
3	The CIA once attempted to kill Fidel Castro with a poisonous cigar.	**FACT** CRaP
4	*Matlock* took place in a fictional San Francisco neighborhood.	**FACT** CRaP
5	On *Frasier*, the name of Mr. Crane's dog is Freddie.	**FACT** CRaP

(FACT) for correct answer, (CRaP) for incorrect answer.

SCORE:

Game One - Total

Who will be included into the Hall of Fame or Shame?
Add up all rounds to find out this game's winner.

Team A	Team B
Round 1 (+ bonus points):	Round 1 (+ bonus points):
Round 2 (+ bonus points):	Round 2 (+ bonus points):
Rush Hour:	Rush Hour:
Total:	Total:

Put yourself into the Hall of Fame or Hall of Shame on pages 174 and 175.

Game Two

If in doubt, guess. The fact is you still have a 50/50 chance of getting it right. Team B reads the questions first and don't forget to add bonus points when checking your answers. Here's Game 2!

Team A - Round 1

Team B, get ready to ask Team A these five questions. Every correct answer is worth one point. Get all five right and score a bonus 2 points.

1	Michael Jackson purchased the skeleton of the Elephant Man, John Merrick.	**FACT** CRaP
2	Marge Simpson and Jacqueline Kennedy share a maiden name.	**FACT** CRaP
3	The B52's band name derived from frontman Fred Schneider's plane fascination.	**FACT** CRaP
4	Tiger Woods was the 1st African-American to play the Masters Tournament in Augusta, GA.	**FACT** CRaP
5	Edgar Allen Poe lied about his age to enter the U.S. Army.	**FACT** CRaP

FACT for correct answer, **CRaP** for incorrect answer.

SCORE:

Team B - Round 1

Team A, get ready to ask Team B these five questions. Every correct answer is worth one point. Get all five right and score a bonus 2 points.

1	*Stracchino* is an Italian cheese.	**FACT** CRaP
2	The 1947 movie Casablanca was filmed in Morocco.	**FACT** CRaP
3	The Popsicle was invented by mistake by an 11 year old.	**FACT** CRaP
4	The fig is known as a "rich man's food" in the Middle East.	**FACT** CRaP
5	'80s band *Frankie Goes to Hollywood* once went by the name *Hollycaust.*	**FACT** CRaP

FACT for correct answer, **CRaP** for incorrect answer.

SCORE:

Team A - Round 2

Team B, get ready to ask Team A these five questions. Every correct answer is worth one point. Get all five right and score a bonus 2 points.

1	Mustard contains lycopene, a cancer-fighting agent.	**FACT** CRaP
2	A McDonald's Quarter Pounder with Cheese contains 30 grams of fat.	**FACT** CRaP
3	Squid is a favorite pizza topper in Japan.	**FACT** CRaP
4	Paris' Notre Dame is the largest Gothic cathedral.	**FACT** CRaP
5	Patrick Swayze was once involved in a plane crash.	**FACT** CRaP

FACT for correct answer, **CRaP** for incorrect answer.

SCORE:

Team B - Round 2

Team A, get ready to ask Team B these five questions. Every correct answer is worth one point. Get all five right and score a bonus 2 points.

1	Rapper Slick Rick is known as *The Ruler*.	**FACT** CRaP
2	Andrew Johnson was first to employ the Democratic "Donkey" symbol.	**FACT** CRaP
3	Begun in 1882, Gaudi's famous *Sagrada Familia* cathedral is still under construction.	**FACT** CRaP
4	The assassination of Franz Ferdinand triggered the start of WWII.	**FACT** CRaP
5	Beavertail is a favorite ballpark food for Montreal Expos fans.	**FACT** CRaP

(**FACT**) for correct answer, (CRaP) for incorrect answer.

SCORE:

Team A - Rush Hour

Team B, get ready to call out the questions. Answer all questions correctly for 10 points, but get just one wrong and you score zilch.

1	Motorola launched the first cell phone call in 1973.	**FACT** CRaP
2	Arnold Palmer's first professional win was at the Canadian Open.	**FACT** CRaP
3	Hitting three home runs in one game is called a *Golden Sombrero*.	**FACT** CRaP
4	Frida Kahlo married Diego Rivera - twice.	**FACT** CRaP
5	The New York Giants won the first NFL championship game in 1933.	**FACT** CRaP

FACT for correct answer, CRaP for incorrect answer.

SCORE:

Team B - Rush Hour

Team A, get ready to call out the questions. Answer all questions correctly for 10 points, but get just one wrong and you score zilch.

1	Cuban nationalists killed Ernest Hemmingway in 1963.	**FACT** CRaP
2	The Woodstock Music and Arts Festival didn't take place in Woodstock.	**FACT** CRaP
3	The first Mormon temple was dedicated in Salt Lake City.	**FACT** CRaP
4	The Purple Heart is the oldest recognized military decoration.	**FACT** CRaP
5	New York was the first capital of the United States.	**FACT** CRaP

FACT for correct answer, **CRaP** for incorrect answer.

SCORE:

Game Two - Total

It's time to add up your scores, including all bonus points and see who's full of Crap.

Team A
Round 1 (+ bonus points):
Round 2 (+ bonus points):
Rush Hour:
Total:

Team B
Round 1 (+ bonus points):
Round 2 (+ bonus points):
Rush Hour:
Total:

The Hall of Fame or Shame awaits your scores on pages 174 and 175.

Game Three

A lot of the answers in this game are actually Crap. And that's a Fact!

Team A - Round 1

Team B, get ready to ask Team A these five questions. Every correct answer is worth one point. Get all five right and score a bonus 2 points.

1	Robert Duvall spoke the famous phrase: "I love the smell of napalm in the morning."	**FACT** CRaP
2	The *Mona Lisa* was Michelangelo's most famous work.	**FACT** CRaP
3	The Statue of Liberty's nose measures five feet.	**FACT** CRaP
4	*Linguine* literally translates as "little tongues."	**FACT** CRaP
5	Impressionist painter Claude Monet went blind in his teens.	**FACT** CRaP

(**FACT**) for correct answer, (CRaP) for incorrect answer.

SCORE:

Team B - Round 1

Team A, get ready to ask Team B these five questions. Every correct answer is worth one point. Get all five right and score a bonus 2 points.

1	The first Starbucks opened in North Beach, San Francisco.	**FACT** CRaP
2	Uncle Sam was an idea created by Abraham Lincoln to increase patriotism.	**FACT** CRaP
3	Andy Warhol created over 600 films in his lifetime.	**FACT** CRaP
4	*Exquisite corpse* is the name of a surrealist game.	**FACT** CRaP
5	The Magna Carta was signed in 1215.	**FACT** CRaP

(**FACT**) for correct answer, (CRaP) for incorrect answer.

SCORE:

Team A - Round 2

Team B, get ready to ask Team A these five questions. Every correct answer is worth one point. Get all five right and score a bonus 2 points.

1	Pennsylvania was the first state to ratify the Constitution.	**FACT** CRaP
2	Fire extinguishers use fuel and oxygen to put out fires.	**FACT** CRaP
3	Most toothpaste brands contain saccharin.	**FACT** CRaP
4	Trouble instigators on internet message boards are referred to as gnomes.	**FACT** CRaP
5	An Englishman invented the Rubik's Cube.	**FACT** CRaP

FACT for correct answer, CRaP for incorrect answer. | SCORE:

Team B - Round 2

Team A, get ready to ask Team B these five questions. Every correct answer is worth one point. Get all five right and score a bonus 2 points.

1	Raccoons are nocturnal.	**FACT** CRaP
2	A Gibson is a martini garnished with a pickled onion.	**FACT** CRaP
3	*The New York Times* is nicknamed the "puce goose."	**FACT** CRaP
4	A "lich" is otherwise known as a type of undead creature.	**FACT** CRaP
5	A science fiction writer founded the Church of Scientology.	**FACT** CRaP

FACT for correct answer, CRaP for incorrect answer.　　SCORE:

Team A - Rush Hour

Team B, get ready to call out the questions. Answer all questions correctly for 10 points, but get just one wrong and you score zilch.

1	Aphrodite is the Roman goddess of love.	**FACT** CRaP
2	The Pope serves as Head of State of Vatican City.	**FACT** CRaP
3	John F. Kennedy had a pony named Leprechaun.	**FACT** CRaP
4	A human's large intestine can measure up to 21 feet long.	**FACT** CRaP
5	Poor hydration can cause wrinkles.	**FACT** CRaP

FACT for correct answer, CRaP for incorrect answer.

SCORE:

Team B - Rush Hour

Team A, get ready to call out the questions. Answer all questions correctly for 10 points, but get just one wrong and you score zilch.

1	A raisin is a dried fruit version of a plum.	**FACT** CRaP
2	The Great Wall of China is visible from outer space.	**FACT** CRaP
3	Mont Blanc is the highest peak in Austria.	**FACT** CRaP
4	The clavicle is the dangly flesh between your tonsils.	**FACT** CRaP
5	The maple leaf on the Canadian flag has three leaves.	**FACT** CRaP

(**FACT**) for correct answer, (CRaP) for incorrect answer.

SCORE:

Game Three - Total

There are only two answers in this game and only two places for your name!

Team A	Team B
Round 1 (+ bonus points):	**Round 1 (+ bonus points):**
Round 2 (+ bonus points):	**Round 2 (+ bonus points):**
Rush Hour:	**Rush Hour:**
Total:	**Total:**

See pages 174 and 175 and put your name where it belongs.

Game Four

They say an ounce of facts is worth
a ton of arguments. What a lot of Crap.

Team A - Round 1

Team B, get ready to ask Team A these five questions. Every correct answer is worth one point. Get all five right and score a bonus 2 points.

1	The *Spirit of Justice* statue features a woman with one breast exposed.	**FACT** CRaP
2	In Shakespeare's time, all of his character roles were played by men.	**FACT** CRaP
3	Dressage refers to a specific, competitive equestrian style.	**FACT** CRaP
4	Movie director Richard Linklater coined the term "*slacker*."	**FACT** CRaP
5	Lou Reed graduated with high academic honors from Syracuse University.	**FACT** CRaP

FACT for correct answer, **CRaP** for incorrect answer.

SCORE:

Team B - Round 1

Team A, get ready to ask Team B these five questions. Every correct answer is worth one point. Get all five right and score a bonus 2 points.

1	Uni is the Japanese name for the edible portion of a sea urchin.	**FACT** CRaP
2	Wayne Gretsky was the first NHL player to score 50 goals in 50 games.	**FACT** CRaP
3	Kennedy's campaign slogan promised "a chicken in every pot."	**FACT** CRaP
4	Krishna is a Hindu deity.	**FACT** CRaP
5	Kanshi is the Korean version of haiku.	**FACT** CRaP

(**FACT**) for correct answer, (CRaP) for incorrect answer.

SCORE:

Team A - Round 2

Team B, get ready to ask Team A these five questions. Every correct answer is worth one point. Get all five right and score a bonus 2 points.

1	Picasso's *Guernica* commemorates the Nazi bombing of a Basque city.	**FACT** CRaP
2	Homer Simpson ran for office with the slogan "Can't someone else do it?"	**FACT** CRaP
3	Dionysus is the Greek god of wine.	**FACT** CRaP
4	Cats can't get rabies.	**FACT** CRaP
5	John Keats was buried in the UK's Heptonstall Churchyard.	**FACT** CRaP

FACT for correct answer, **CRaP** for incorrect answer.

SCORE:

ANSWERS: 1) FACT 2) FACT 3) FACT 4) FACT 5) CRAP

Team B - Round 2

Team A, get ready to ask Team B these five questions. Every correct answer is worth one point. Get all five right and score a bonus 2 points.

1	George Foreman named all five of his sons George Foreman.	**FACT** CRaP
2	The Statue of Liberty tips the scales at 225 tons.	**FACT** CRaP
3	In theater, the "fourth wall" refers to the audience.	**FACT** CRaP
4	Plato and Aristotle both appear in Raphael's painting, *The School of Athens*.	**FACT** CRaP
5	Trix breakfast cereal is composed of 46% sugar.	**FACT** CRaP

FACT for correct answer, CRaP for incorrect answer.

SCORE:

Team A - Rush Hour

Team B, get ready to call out the questions. Answer all questions correctly for 10 points, but get just one wrong and you score zilch.

1	Disneyworld scored the title of "America's Most Beautiful Theme Park" for the last 15 years.	**FACT** CRaP
2	Sydney is Australia's capital.	**FACT** CRaP
3	The Tigris River flows through Baghdad.	**FACT** CRaP
4	Magic Johnson was the first American celebrity to come forward as having AIDS.	**FACT** CRaP
5	Delaware is the only U.S. state that does not feature a national park.	**FACT** CRaP

FACT for correct answer, **CRaP** for incorrect answer.

SCORE:

ANSWERS: 1) CRAP 2) CRAP 3) FACT 4) CRAP 5) FACT

Team B - Rush Hour

Team A, get ready to call out the questions. Answer all questions correctly for 10 points, but get just one wrong and you score zilch.

1	Betsy Ross was the founder of the American Red Cross.	**FACT** CRaP
2	Baskin-Robbins once created an ice cream flavor called "Lunar Cheesecake."	**FACT** CRaP
3	Yosemite is the oldest national park in the U.S.	**FACT** CRaP
4	Kwame Brown was the #1 NBA draft pick in 2000.	**FACT** CRaP
5	Brazil is the largest country in South America	**FACT** CRaP

(FACT) for correct answer, (CRaP) for incorrect answer.

SCORE:

ANSWERS: 1) CRAP 2) FACT 3) CRAP 4) FACT 5) FACT

37

Game Four - Total

Success is determined only by your ability to pick Fact from Crap. It's time to add up your scores.

Team A
Round 1 (+ bonus points):
Round 2 (+ bonus points):
Rush Hour:
Total:

Team B
Round 1 (+ bonus points):
Round 2 (+ bonus points):
Rush Hour:
Total:

The Hall of Fame or Shame awaits you on pages 174 and 175.

Game Five

Most successes are built on a multitude of failures.
So how are you doing so far?

Team A - Round 1

Team B, get ready to ask Team A these five questions. Every correct answer is worth one point. Get all five right and score a bonus 2 points.

1	The *occipital* bone is located in the foot.	**FACT** CRaP
2	A *rhyzome* is four-sided geometrical shape.	**FACT** CRaP
3	The Seattle Space Needle is the tallest free-standing observation tower in the U.S.	**FACT** CRaP
4	The *"AFQT"* refers to the test given to new Armed Forces recruits.	**FACT** CRaP
5	Japan was the first non-U.S. team to win the Little League World Series.	**FACT** CRaP

(**FACT**) for correct answer, (CRaP) for incorrect answer.

SCORE:

Team B - Round 1

Team A, get ready to ask Team B these five questions. Every correct answer is worth one point. Get all five right and score a bonus 2 points.

1	The Civil War resulted in more U.S. soldier casualties than any other wars.	**FACT** CRaP
2	Noah practiced winemaking in Biblical days.	**FACT** CRaP
3	Mary, Queen of Scots, was an avid golfer.	**FACT** CRaP
4	Depeche mode literally translates into "depressed manner" in French.	**FACT** CRaP
5	Mazel means luck in Yiddish.	**FACT** CRaP

FACT for correct answer, **CRaP** for incorrect answer.

SCORE:

Team A - Round 2

Team B, get ready to ask Team A these five questions. Every correct answer is worth one point. Get all five right and score a bonus 2 points.

1	Kansas is nicknamed the *Show-Me State*.	**FACT** CRaP
2	Nirvana's *Nevermind* was released in 1991.	**FACT** CRaP
3	The first Hershey Kiss was introduced in 1909.	**FACT** CRaP
4	*Dharma* refers to a specific form of meditative yoga.	**FACT** CRaP
5	Black-eyed peas are not peas.	**FACT** CRaP

(**FACT**) for correct answer, (**CRaP**) for incorrect answer.

SCORE:

Team B - Round 2

Team A, get ready to ask Team B these five questions. Every correct answer is worth one point. Get all five right and score a bonus 2 points.

1	Ancient Egyptians placed their hands on onions when taking oaths.	**FACT** CRaP
2	A *drupe* is a fruit with a hard seed or stone encased in flesh.	**FACT** CRaP
3	A *bear market* is associated with optimism and investor confidence.	**FACT** CRaP
4	The cube root of 64 is 4.	**FACT** CRaP
5	A *canzone* is a baked Italian treat.	**FACT** CRaP

FACT for correct answer, **CRaP** for incorrect answer.

SCORE:

Team A - Rush Hour

Team B, get ready to call out the questions. Answer all questions correctly for 10 points, but get just one wrong and you score zilch.

1	A *palindrome* is a word that reads the same backwards and forwards.	**FACT** CRaP
2	*Mania* is a mood disorder characterized by severe depression.	**FACT** CRaP
3	They Might Be Giants recorded a children's album.	**FACT** CRaP
4	Your thalamus is located in your heart cavity.	**FACT** CRaP
5	On *Black Monday*, the Dow Jones Industrial Average plunged 508 points.	**FACT** CRaP

FACT for correct answer, **CRaP** for incorrect answer.

SCORE:

Team B - Rush Hour

Team A, get ready to call out the questions. Answer all questions correctly for 10 points, but get just one wrong and you score zilch.

1	The Rorschach test measures intelligence.	**FACT** CRaP
2	White was considered the color of mourning in 16th century France.	**FACT** CRaP
3	Willie Nelson did the voice-overs in the Dukes of Hazard.	**FACT** CRaP
4	Memes are passed between people like viruses.	**FACT** CRaP
5	A woman's first menstrual cycle is referred to as menarche.	**FACT** CRaP

(**FACT**) for correct answer, (CRaP) for incorrect answer.

SCORE:

Game Five - Total

FACT: It's not that difficult – there are only two answers to choose from!

Team A	Team B
Round 1 (+ bonus points):	Round 1 (+ bonus points):
Round 2 (+ bonus points):	Round 2 (+ bonus points):
Rush Hour:	Rush Hour:
Total:	Total:

So how did you score? Permanently inscribe your names where they belong.
Is it the Hall of Fame, or the sorry Hall of Shame?

Game Six

Come on now, use your brain. It's the little things that count ... and that's a Fact.

Team A - Round 1

Team B, get ready to ask Team A these five questions. Every correct answer is worth one point. Get all five right and score a bonus 2 points.

1	Narcolepsy is a sexual disorder.	**FACT** CRaP
2	An ear of corn always has an even number of rows.	**FACT** CRaP
3	The Las Vegas version of the Phantom of the Opera added two musical numbers.	**FACT** CRaP
4	Walt Disney had a dog named Pluto.	**FACT** CRaP
5	Clay is what makes glossy paper glossy.	**FACT** CRaP

(FACT) for correct answer, (CRaP) for incorrect answer.

SCORE:

ANSWERS: 1) CRAP 2) FACT 3) CRAP 4) CRAP 5) FACT

Team B - Round 1

Team A, get ready to ask Team B these five questions. Every correct answer is worth one point. Get all five right and score a bonus 2 points.

1	Michael Jackson has a son called Towel.	**FACT** CRaP
2	The White House has 200 rooms.	**FACT** CRaP
3	Fingerprints develop on a child within the first trimester.	**FACT** CRaP
4	Apples are Americans' favorite fruit.	**FACT** CRaP
5	The words month and silver possess no English language rhyme.	**FACT** CRaP

FACT for correct answer, **CRaP** for incorrect answer.

SCORE:

Team A - Round 2

Team B, get ready to ask Team A these five questions. Every correct answer is worth one point. Get all five right and score a bonus 2 points.

1	John is the most common name in the world.	**FACT** CRaP
2	The plastic thing at the end of a shoelace is called an aglet.	**FACT** CRaP
3	No two spider webs are the same.	**FACT** CRaP
4	90% of all humans live on 83% of Earth's land.	**FACT** CRaP
5	Friday the 13ths occur whenever a month begins on a Sunday.	**FACT** CRaP

(**FACT**) for correct answer, (**CRaP**) for incorrect answer.

SCORE:

Team B - Round 2

Team A, get ready to ask Team B these five questions. Every correct answer is worth one point. Get all five right and score a bonus 2 points.

1	Sharks cause more human deaths than any other animal.	**FACT** CRaP
2	50% of bank robberies occur on Fridays.	**FACT** CRaP
3	The spider plant is also known as the airplane plant.	**FACT** CRaP
4	Elvis' "Jailhouse Rock" was the first rock and roll song to hit #1 on the charts.	**FACT** CRaP
5	The Nile is the world's longest river.	**FACT** CRaP

FACT for correct answer, **CRaP** for incorrect answer.

SCORE:

Team A - Rush Hour

Team B, get ready to call out the questions. Answer all questions correctly for 10 points, but get just one wrong and you score zilch.

1	The *Explorer* was the first American satellite to orbit the Earth.	**FACT** CRaP
2	Kelvar Swatch invented the first wristwatch in 1880.	**FACT** CRaP
3	Cambodia boasts the world's largest alphabet.	**FACT** CRaP
4	Traces of cocaine were found on UK bank notes in 2000.	**FACT** CRaP
5	Hot dogs are American's favorite amusement park snack.	**FACT** CRaP

FACT for correct answer, **CRaP** for incorrect answer.

SCORE:

Team B - Rush Hour

Team A, get ready to call out the questions. Answer all questions correctly for 10 points, but get just one wrong and you score zilch.

1	A woman's heart beats faster than a man's.	**FACT** CRaP
2	It takes more muscles to smile than it does to frown.	**FACT** CRaP
3	Pike's Peak is the tallest mountain in the continental U.S.	**FACT** CRaP
4	The University of Delaware's mascot is a blue hen.	**FACT** CRaP
5	"Onion" comes from a Latin word meaning large pearl.	**FACT** CRaP

FACT for correct answer, CRaP for incorrect answer.　　SCORE:

Game Six - Total

Who will be included into the Hall of Fame or Shame?
Add up all rounds to find out this game's winner.

Team A	Team B
Round 1 (+ bonus points):	Round 1 (+ bonus points):
Round 2 (+ bonus points):	Round 2 (+ bonus points):
Rush Hour:	Rush Hour:
Total:	Total:

Put yourself into the Hall of Fame or Hall of Shame on pages 174 and 175.

Game Seven

Let's face facts. If you're not getting 50% correct, it's time to start guessing.

Team A - Round 1

Team B, get ready to ask Team A these five questions. Every correct answer is worth one point. Get all five right and score a bonus 2 points.

1	Music composer John Cage is famous for a performance featuring silence.	**FACT** CRaP
2	Cows have a half dozen stomachs.	**FACT** CRaP
3	*Tagliatelle* is Italian slang for stupid troll.	**FACT** CRaP
4	*Agape* is a Greek term for love.	**FACT** CRaP
5	Laissez fair economics is opposed to government intervention in business.	**FACT** CRaP

(**FACT**) for correct answer, (**CRaP**) for incorrect answer.

SCORE:

Team B - Round 1

Team A, get ready to ask Team B these five questions. Every correct answer is worth one point. Get all five right and score a bonus 2 points.

1	The musical *Cats* was based on an Andrew Lloyd Webber poem.	**FACT** CRaP
2	The famous *Kinsey Report* was an extensive study on human sexual behavior.	**FACT** CRaP
3	102 is the "median" in the following series: 1, 100, 102, 456, and 789.	**FACT** CRaP
4	An elegy is generally read at a baptism.	**FACT** CRaP
5	*Nudnik* means "pest" in Yiddish.	**FACT** CRaP

FACT for correct answer, CRaP for incorrect answer.

SCORE:

Team A - Round 2

Team B, get ready to ask Team A these five questions. Every correct answer is worth one point. Get all five right and score a bonus 2 points.

1	The *cones* in your eyes help you see color.	**FACT** CRaP
2	The first U.S. space shuttle to enter space was the *Challenger*.	**FACT** CRaP
3	Ohio is the "*Hawkeye state*".	**FACT** CRaP
4	Heroin is an opiate.	**FACT** CRaP
5	A conceit can be a type of metaphor.	**FACT** CRaP

FACT for correct answer, **CRaP** for incorrect answer.

SCORE:

Team B - Round 2

Team A, get ready to ask Team B these five questions. Every correct answer is worth one point. Get all five right and score a bonus 2 points.

1	REM sleep is the period when your brain is the least active.	**FACT** CRaP
2	Capital gain is profits made from asset value appreciation.	**FACT** CRaP
3	The magnolia is Louisiana's state flower.	**FACT** CRaP
4	*Acrophobia* is a fear of spiders.	**FACT** CRaP
5	Ronald Reagan's first wife starred on Dallas in the '80s.	**FACT** CRaP

FACT for correct answer, CRaP for incorrect answer.

SCORE:

Team A - Rush Hour

Team B, get ready to call out the questions. Answer all questions correctly for 10 points, but get just one wrong and you score zilch.

1	George Michael's *Faith* was the #1 song for 1987.	**FACT** CRaP
2	It took three ax whacks to decapitate Mary Queen of Scots.	**FACT** CRaP
3	*Assonance* is a repetition of vowel sounds.	**FACT** CRaP
4	People suffering from aphasia can't walk.	**FACT** CRaP
5	Kim Gordon fronted the band "Hole."	**FACT** CRaP

FACT for correct answer, CRaP for incorrect answer.

SCORE:

Team B - Rush Hour

Team A, get ready to call out the questions. Answer all questions correctly for 10 points, but get just one wrong and you score zilch.

1	Whiskey was first brewed in 1820.	**FACT** CRaP
2	A fertilized human egg is called a zygote.	**FACT** CRaP
3	ET's favorite candy was Skittles.	**FACT** CRaP
4	The word sushi actually refers to the rice.	**FACT** CRaP
5	Post Civil War morphine addiction was referred to as Soldier's Disease.	**FACT** CRaP

FACT for correct answer, **CRaP** for incorrect answer.

SCORE:

Game Seven - Total

It's time to add up your scores, including all bonus points and see who's full of Crap.

Team A
Round 1 (+ bonus points):
Round 2 (+ bonus points):
Rush Hour:
Total:

Team B
Round 1 (+ bonus points):
Round 2 (+ bonus points):
Rush Hour:
Total:

The Hall of Fame or Shame awaits your scores on pages 174 and 175.

Game Eight

Remember, fame or shame awaits you
at the end of every game.

Team A - Round 1

Team B, get ready to ask Team A these five questions. Every correct answer is worth one point. Get all five right and score a bonus 2 points.

1	It is possible to kill yourself by holding your breath.	**FACT** CRaP
2	Elvis is one of the world's top posthumous money-earners.	**FACT** CRaP
3	Ants sleep 16 hours a day.	**FACT** CRaP
4	Tiger Woods won the 2004 U.S. Open golf championship.	**FACT** CRaP
5	The *acetylcholine* (ACh) is a common type of neurotransmitter.	**FACT** CRaP

FACT for correct answer, **CRaP** for incorrect answer.

SCORE:

Team B - Round 1

Team A, get ready to ask Team B these five questions. Every correct answer is worth one point. Get all five right and score a bonus 2 points.

1	"Average" and "mean" are the same thing, mathematically.	**FACT** CRaP
2	Shakespeare wrote: "How do I love thee? Let me count the ways."	**FACT** CRaP
3	Actress Esther Williams was also a competitive swimmer.	**FACT** CRaP
4	Masochists derive pleasure only from hurting others.	**FACT** CRaP
5	Your *medulla* controls your breathing, heart rate and blood pressure.	**FACT** CRaP

FACT for correct answer, **CRaP** for incorrect answer.

SCORE:

Team A - Round 2

Team B, get ready to ask Team A these five questions. Every correct answer is worth one point. Get all five right and score a bonus 2 points.

1	Three major bodies of water border India.	**FACT** CRaP
2	The gorilla's gestation period is 13 months.	**FACT** CRaP
3	The Paleolithic era, or Old Stone Age, lasted over a million years.	**FACT** CRaP
4	Type A blood is the most popular type worldwide.	**FACT** CRaP
5	Paula Abdul was a Laker girl.	**FACT** CRaP

(FACT) for correct answer, (CRaP) for incorrect answer.

SCORE:

Team B - Round 2

Team A, get ready to ask Team B these five questions. Every correct answer is worth one point. Get all five right and score a bonus 2 points.

1	Ataxia is a medical condition affecting a body's movement.	**FACT** CRaP
2	California is the "*sunshine*" state.	**FACT** CRaP
3	Lorne Michaels founded CNN, the world's largest cable news channel.	**FACT** CRaP
4	Canada is the second largest country in the world.	**FACT** CRaP
5	"*Qualitative*" data is that which is numerical in nature.	**FACT** CRaP

FACT for correct answer, **CRaP** for incorrect answer.

SCORE:

Team A - Rush Hour

Team B, get ready to call out the questions. Answer all questions correctly for 10 points, but get just one wrong and you score zilch.

1	Sao Paolo is Brazil's largest city.	**FACT** CRaP
2	Penguins can't jump.	**FACT** CRaP
3	In economic terms, GNP stands for "goods nationally produced."	**FACT** CRaP
4	Alligators can't move backwards.	**FACT** CRaP
5	Moisture inside the shell is what causes popcorn to pop.	**FACT** CRaP

FACT for correct answer, **CRaP** for incorrect answer.

SCORE:

ANSWERS: 1) FACT 2) CRAP 3) CRAP 4) FACT 5) FACT

Team B - Rush Hour

Team A, get ready to call out the questions. Answer all questions correctly for 10 points, but get just one wrong and you score zilch.

1	The term *schema* refers to a movie's plot structure.	**FACT** CRaP
2	Peonies require ants to bloom.	**FACT** CRaP
3	Super-hit reality TV show *American Idol* hit airwaves in 2002.	**FACT** CRaP
4	Humans cannot dream during REM sleep.	**FACT** CRaP
5	Dahlias are a form of root tuber.	**FACT** CRaP

FACT for correct answer, CRaP for incorrect answer.

SCORE:

Game Eight - Total

There are only two answers in this game and only two places for your name!

Team A	Team B
Round 1 (+ bonus points):	Round 1 (+ bonus points):
Round 2 (+ bonus points):	Round 2 (+ bonus points):
Rush Hour:	Rush Hour:
Total:	Total:

See pages 174 and 175 and put your name where it belongs.

Game Nine

You should be able to sniff out the crap by now.
Let's see who's full of it in Game 9.

Team A - Round 1

Team B, get ready to ask Team A these five questions. Every correct answer is worth one point. Get all five right and score a bonus 2 points.

1	The human liver weighs 9 ounces.	**FACT** CRaP
2	Cashew nuts contain a poisonous oil.	**FACT** CRaP
3	Cappuccino is made of espresso, milk and cocoa.	**FACT** CRaP
4	*Keynesian* economic theory supports government intervention to ensure economic growth.	**FACT** CRaP
5	Barbie's first career was as a teen fashion model.	**FACT** CRaP

FACT for correct answer, **CRaP** for incorrect answer.

SCORE:

ANSWERS: 1) CRAP 2) FACT 3) CRAP 4) FACT 5) FACT

Team B - Round 1

Team A, get ready to ask Team B these five questions. Every correct answer is worth one point. Get all five right and score a bonus 2 points.

1	Thomas Jefferson's face is not featured on Mt. Rushmore.	**FACT** CRaP
2	Letters in Braille are referred to as cells.	**FACT** CRaP
3	It is proper etiquette to rub wooden chopsticks together prior to sushi arrival.	**FACT** CRaP
4	Modern pianos have 88 keys.	**FACT** CRaP
5	The white part of the egg is called the "glair"	**FACT** CRaP

FACT for correct answer, CRaP for incorrect answer.

SCORE:

Team A - Round 2

Team B, get ready to ask Team A these five questions. Every correct answer is worth one point. Get all five right and score a bonus 2 points.

1	Ducks have no eyelids.	**FACT** CRaP
2	In *Cats*, Grizabella is the withered, old cat that sings *Memory*.	**FACT** CRaP
3	Paris Hilton's pug is named Twinkles.	**FACT** CRaP
4	The USSR boycotted the 1984 Olympic games in L.A.	**FACT** CRaP
5	SPAM, the canned meat, contains less than 1 gram of fat per serving.	**FACT** CRaP

(**FACT**) for correct answer, (CRaP) for incorrect answer.

SCORE:

ANSWERS: 1) CRAP 2) FACT 3) CRAP 4) FACT 5) CRAP

Team B - Round 2

Team A, get ready to ask Team B these five questions. Every correct answer is worth one point. Get all five right and score a bonus 2 points.

1	You share your birthday with over 9 million people worldwide.	**FACT** CRaP
2	A rival artist disfigured Raphael.	**FACT** CRaP
3	The '#' symbol is called an "octothorpe."	**FACT** CRaP
4	OJ Simpson was the only college football player to win the Heisman twice.	**FACT** CRaP
5	30% of the earth's surface is ocean.	**FACT** CRaP

FACT for correct answer, **CRaP** for incorrect answer.

SCORE:

Team A - Rush Hour

Team B, get ready to call out the questions. Answer all questions correctly for 10 points, but get just one wrong and you score zilch.

1	The Hoover Dam was built to last 2,000 years.	**FACT** CRaP
2	*Wicked* is a Broadway musical based on Dante's *Inferno*.	**FACT** CRaP
3	A German immigrant arranged the first US nudist event.	**FACT** CRaP
4	An average red blood cell survives 3 days.	**FACT** CRaP
5	Nabokov's *Lolita* was first published in Paris.	**FACT** CRaP

(**FACT**) for correct answer, (CRaP) for incorrect answer.

SCORE:

Team B - Rush Hour

Team A, get ready to call out the questions. Answer all questions correctly for 10 points, but get just one wrong and you score zilch.

1	Portland, Oregon is the western-most city in the continental US.	**FACT** CRaP
2	The underside of the horse's hoof is called the frog.	**FACT** CRaP
3	Robert Wrigley created the first chewing gum in 1907.	**FACT** CRaP
4	Mozart was a freemason.	**FACT** CRaP
5	There are 100 islands in the Philippines.	**FACT** CRaP

FACT for correct answer, **CRaP** for incorrect answer.

SCORE:

Game Nine - Total

Success is determined only by your ability to pick Fact from Crap.
It's time to add up your scores.

Team A
Round 1 (+ bonus points):
Round 2 (+ bonus points):
Rush Hour:
Total:

Team B
Round 1 (+ bonus points):
Round 2 (+ bonus points):
Rush Hour:
Total:

The Hall of Fame or Shame awaits you on pages 174 and 175.

Game Ten

This is no help at all, but a lot of facts started life as Crap. I mean, who knew the world was round?

Team A - Round 1

Team B, get ready to ask Team A these five questions. Every correct answer is worth one point. Get all five right and score a bonus 2 points.

1	In economic terms, "fiat" money refers to debt.	**FACT** CRaP
2	PET scans study the brain.	**FACT** CRaP
3	April is National Poetry Month.	**FACT** CRaP
4	Your nose stops growing around age 25.	**FACT** CRaP
5	Norma Talmadge made the first footprints on Hollywood's Walk of Fame.	**FACT** CRaP

FACT for correct answer, **CRaP** for incorrect answer.

SCORE:

Team B - Round 1

Team A, get ready to ask Team B these five questions. Every correct answer is worth one point. Get all five right and score a bonus 2 points.

1	*Who's Afraid of Virginia Woolf* won the 1963 Pulitzer Prize.	**FACT** CRaP
2	Two and a half million new red blood cells are produced every second.	**FACT** CRaP
3	Pennsylvania is known as the "Constitution State."	**FACT** CRaP
4	Decibels measure sound.	**FACT** CRaP
5	The Ford Mustang was the best-selling car in 1983.	**FACT** CRaP

FACT for correct answer, **CRaP** for incorrect answer.

SCORE:

Team A - Round 2

Team B, get ready to ask Team A these five questions. Every correct answer is worth one point. Get all five right and score a bonus 2 points.

1	Polaris is another name for the north star.	**FACT** CRaP
2	The Walsh family moved to Beverly Hills 90210 from Missouri.	**FACT** CRaP
3	In Panama, the sun rises on the Pacific Ocean.	**FACT** CRaP
4	Emily Dickenson published nearly 1000 poems in her lifetime.	**FACT** CRaP
5	The gluteus maximus is your body's largest muscle.	**FACT** CRaP

FACT for correct answer, **CRaP** for incorrect answer.

SCORE:

ANSWERS: 1) FACT 2) CRAP 3) FACT 4) CRAP 5) FACT

Team B - Round 2

Team A, get ready to ask Team B these five questions. Every correct answer is worth one point. Get all five right and score a bonus 2 points.

1	Mount Everest declines a bit in height every year.	**FACT** CRaP
2	There is no McDonald's in Montpelier, Vermont.	**FACT** CRaP
3	A person from Glasgow is called a Glasgower.	**FACT** CRaP
4	Mafia is an island off of Tanzania.	**FACT** CRaP
5	Caterpillars have more muscles than humans.	**FACT** CRaP

(**FACT**) for correct answer, (CRaP) for incorrect answer.

SCORE:

Team A - Rush Hour

Team B, get ready to call out the questions. Answer all questions correctly for 10 points, but get just one wrong and you score zilch.

1	The musical term *adagio* means 'fast.'	**FACT** CRaP
2	Pineapples belong to the berry family.	**FACT** CRaP
3	Tennessee is bordered by eight states.	**FACT** CRaP
4	Coney Island, New York, is named for its famous ice cream, the *coney*.	**FACT** CRaP
5	Ducks have three eyelids.	**FACT** CRaP

(**FACT**) for correct answer, (CRaP) for incorrect answer.

SCORE:

Team B - Rush Hour

Team A, get ready to call out the questions. Answer all questions correctly for 10 points, but get just one wrong and you score zilch.

1	Hemingway's longest sentence boasted 424 words.	**FACT** CRaP
2	John Keats' early death was blamed on a bad review.	**FACT** CRaP
3	*Help!* was the longest lasting chart-topper for the Beatles.	**FACT** CRaP
4	Amsterdam is the tulip growing capital of the world.	**FACT** CRaP
5	Humans lose half their taste buds by age 60.	**FACT** CRaP

FACT for correct answer, CRaP for incorrect answer.

SCORE:

ANSWERS: 1) FACT 2) FACT 3) CRAP 4) CRAP 5) FACT

Game Ten - Total

FACT: It's not that difficult – there are only two answers to choose from!

Team A
Round 1 (+ bonus points):
Round 2 (+ bonus points):
Rush Hour:
Total:

Team B
Round 1 (+ bonus points):
Round 2 (+ bonus points):
Rush Hour:
Total:

So how did you score? Permanently inscribe your names where they belong. Is it the Hall of Fame, or the sorry Hall of Shame?

Game Eleven

There are thirty more brain-teasing
trivia questions coming right up. Good luck!

Team A - Round 1

Team B, get ready to ask Team A these five questions. Every correct answer is worth one point. Get all five right and score a bonus 2 points.

1	The word *Seoul* in Korean translates as "capital."	**FACT** CRaP
2	The bodies of dead workers are buried in Hoover Dam.	**FACT** CRaP
3	*Little House on the Prairie* was set in California.	**FACT** CRaP
4	A "*schlimazel*" means 'unlucky person' in Yiddish.	**FACT** CRaP
5	The peace lily is Britain's favorite houseplant.	**FACT** CRaP

FACT for correct answer, CRaP for incorrect answer.

SCORE:

Team B - Round 1

Team A, get ready to ask Team B these five questions. Every correct answer is worth one point. Get all five right and score a bonus 2 points.

1	The first open heart surgery took place in 1948.	**FACT** CRaP
2	Barry Manilow did not write *I Write the Songs*.	**FACT** CRaP
3	On *Friends*, Phoebe's sister's name is Consuela.	**FACT** CRaP
4	A cat can jump seven times its height.	**FACT** CRaP
5	NASA was established in 1969.	**FACT** CRaP

(**FACT**) for correct answer, (**CRaP**) for incorrect answer.

SCORE:

ANSWERS: 1) CRAP 2) FACT 3) CRAP 4) FACT 5) CRAP

Team A - Round 2

Team B, get ready to ask Team A these five questions. Every correct answer is worth one point. Get all five right and score a bonus 2 points.

1	*Happy Days* spawned four sitcom spin-offs.	**FACT** CRaP
2	CEO stands for Corporate Executive Organizer.	**FACT** CRaP
3	The heaviest kidney stone weighed 12.5oz.	**FACT** CRaP
4	The earth is 93 millions miles away from the moon.	**FACT** CRaP
5	The Vatican City is smaller than New York's Central Park.	**FACT** CRaP

FACT for correct answer, **CRaP** for incorrect answer.

SCORE:

Team B - Round 2

Team A, get ready to ask Team B these five questions. Every correct answer is worth one point. Get all five right and score a bonus 2 points.

1	Siddhartha Gautama founded Islam.	**FACT** CRaP
2	Prior to *the Smiths*, Morrissey was in a punk band called *the Nosebleeds*.	**FACT** CRaP
3	Lorenzo di Medici had his wife Anne Boleyn executed.	**FACT** CRaP
4	Jeremy Irons played Humbert Humbert in the movie version of Nabokov's *Lolita*.	**FACT** CRaP
5	Sly Stone played Vinnie Barbarino on *Welcome Back Kotter*.	**FACT** CRaP

FACT for correct answer, **CRaP** for incorrect answer.

SCORE:

Team A - Rush Hour

Team B, get ready to call out the questions. Answer all questions correctly for 10 points, but get just one wrong and you score zilch.

1	Gertrude Stein once offered Hemingway writing advice, which he accepted.	**FACT** CRaP
2	*Frasier* is a spin-off of the show *Family Ties*.	**FACT** CRaP
3	"Wernicke's" area of the brain is where language skills develop.	**FACT** CRaP
4	The Brady's dog was named Buddy.	**FACT** CRaP
5	The first flight by the Wright Brothers took place in 1903.	**FACT** CRaP

FACT for correct answer, **CRaP** for incorrect answer.

SCORE:

Team B - Rush Hour

Team A, get ready to call out the questions. Answer all questions correctly for 10 points, but get just one wrong and you score zilch.

1	Charles Dickens is the most widely read Romantic novelist.	**FACT** CRaP
2	Oscar Wilde was arrested for indecency.	**FACT** CRaP
3	Green Peace was founded by college undergrads at New York University.	**FACT** CRaP
4	Lincoln's Gettysburg Address starts with a Biblical reference.	**FACT** CRaP
5	Table tennis is not an Olympic sport.	**FACT** CRaP

FACT for correct answer, **CRaP** for incorrect answer.

SCORE:

Game Eleven - Total

Who will be included into the Hall of Fame or Shame?
Add up all rounds to find out this game's winner.

Team A
Round 1 (+ bonus points):
Round 2 (+ bonus points):
Rush Hour:
Total:

Team B
Round 1 (+ bonus points):
Round 2 (+ bonus points):
Rush Hour:
Total:

Put yourself into the Hall of Fame or Hall of Shame on pages 174 and 175.

Game Twelve

It's time to sort the good from the bad, the right from the wrong, the true from the false and the Fact from the Crap.

Team A - Round 1

Team B, get ready to ask Team A these five questions. Every correct answer is worth one point. Get all five right and score a bonus 2 points.

1	Electric eels were once used for electric shock therapy.	**FACT** CRaP
2	Mercury is the smallest of the planets.	**FACT** CRaP
3	Christopher Walken starred in a Broadway musical based on a James Joyce novel.	**FACT** CRaP
4	Garfield's canine nemesis is named Eddie.	**FACT** CRaP
5	Chairman Mao's *Great Leap* was modeled after the Russian economic structure.	**FACT** CRaP

FACT for correct answer, **CRaP** for incorrect answer.

SCORE:

ANSWERS: 1) FACT 2) CRAP 3) FACT 4) CRAP 5) CRAP

Team B - Round 1

Team A, get ready to ask Team B these five questions. Every correct answer is worth one point. Get all five right and score a bonus 2 points.

1	Galileo was condemned by the Catholic Church.	**FACT** CRaP
2	On Jupiter, a "day" lasts under 10 hours.	**FACT** CRaP
3	Kandinsky is considered the father of the Impressionist art movement.	**FACT** CRaP
4	Texas allows absentee ballots submitted from space.	**FACT** CRaP
5	Gertrude Stein is best known for her work, *Mrs. Dalloway*.	**FACT** CRaP

(**FACT**) for correct answer, (CRaP) for incorrect answer.

SCORE:

Team A - Round 2

Team B, get ready to ask Team A these five questions. Every correct answer is worth one point. Get all five right and score a bonus 2 points.

1	Emily Bronte wrote *Wuthering Heights* the same year Marx penned *The Poverty of Philosophy*.	**FACT** CRaP
2	St. Patrick brought Christianity to Ireland.	**FACT** CRaP
3	On the Brady Bunch, Alice's last name is Nelson.	**FACT** CRaP
4	It takes 24 hours for the light from the sun to reach the earth.	**FACT** CRaP
5	On *Beverly Hills 90210*, Brandon Walsh's car was named Mondale.	**FACT** CRaP

FACT for correct answer, **CRaP** for incorrect answer.

SCORE:

ANSWERS: 1) FACT 2) FACT 3) FACT 4) CRAP 5) FACT

Team B - Round 2

Team A, get ready to ask Team B these five questions. Every correct answer is worth one point. Get all five right and score a bonus 2 points.

1	It takes the Earth 365 days to revolve around the sun.	**FACT** CRaP
2	As a schoolteacher, prior to becoming President, James Garfield used a bullwhip to keep order in his classroom.	**FACT** CRaP
3	The first Winter Olympics were held in Athens, Greece.	**FACT** CRaP
4	Puccini wrote his *Madame Butterfly* operatic masterpiece in 1904.	**FACT** CRaP
5	A *farrier* is a person who specializes in ship navigation.	**FACT** CRaP

(FACT) for correct answer, (CRaP) for incorrect answer. SCORE:

Team A - Rush Hour

Team B, get ready to call out the questions. Answer all questions correctly for 10 points, but get just one wrong and you score zilch.

1	Celery takes more calories to eat than it actually contains.	**FACT** CRaP
2	Presidential hopeful Al Gore begged, unsuccessfully, to host *Saturday Night Live*.	**FACT** CRaP
3	If you were a *luthier*, you'd know how to fix guitars.	**FACT** CRaP
4	Actor Mel Gibson landed himself in prison in 2006, for making anti-Semitic threats.	**FACT** CRaP
5	Vanilla comes from orchids.	**FACT** CRaP

FACT for correct answer, **CRaP** for incorrect answer.

SCORE:

ANSWERS: 1) FACT 2) CRAP 3) FACT 4) CRAP 5) FACT

Team B - Rush Hour

Team A, get ready to call out the questions. Answer all questions correctly for 10 points, but get just one wrong and you score zilch.

1	A bears' body temperature will rise during hibernation, keeping it alive.	**FACT** CRaP
2	Willie Nelson's early music instruction came in the form of mail order lessons.	**FACT** CRaP
3	Gazpacho was invented by accident when a Spanish chef forgot to heat a tomato-based soup.	**FACT** CRaP
4	The *Pieta* is the only work that Michelangelo signed.	**FACT** CRaP
5	Sweet wines, like Rieslings, are produced when a mold called *botrytis cinerea* attacks a certain wine varietal.	**FACT** CRaP

(**FACT**) for correct answer, (CRaP) for incorrect answer.   SCORE:

Game Twelve - Total

It's time to add up your scores, including all bonus points and see who's full of Crap.

Team A	Team B
Round 1 (+ bonus points):	Round 1 (+ bonus points):
Round 2 (+ bonus points):	Round 2 (+ bonus points):
Rush Hour:	Rush Hour:
Total:	Total:

The Hall of Fame or Shame awaits your scores on pages 174 and 175.

Game Thirteen

The fact is a lot of people are superstitious about the number 13. Or is it really just Crap?

Team A - Round 1

Team B, get ready to ask Team A these five questions. Every correct answer is worth one point. Get all five right and score a bonus 2 points.

1	Flea, of the band Red Hot Chili Peppers, was born in London.	**FACT** CRaP
2	Bats are basically birds without feathers.	**FACT** CRaP
3	George Lucas' first Star Wars movie hit theaters in 1977.	**FACT** CRaP
4	Homer wrote both the *Iliad* and the *Odyssey*.	**FACT** CRaP
5	An androgynist is a person who dislikes women.	**FACT** CRaP

(**FACT**) for correct answer, (**CRaP**) for incorrect answer.

SCORE:

ANSWERS: 1) CRAP 2) CRAP 3) FACT 4) FACT 5) CRAP

Team B - Round 1

Team A, get ready to ask Team B these five questions. Every correct answer is worth one point. Get all five right and score a bonus 2 points.

1	Buzz, hiss, thump and ker-splat are all examples of onomatopoeia.	**FACT** CRaP
2	Anapest is a suburb of Berlin.	**FACT** CRaP
3	Diabetes is the number one cause of blindness in the US.	**FACT** CRaP
4	A pastoral is a kind of poem typified by sarcasm and dourness.	**FACT** CRaP
5	The word *Islam* literally translates into English as "submission."	**FACT** CRaP

(**FACT**) for correct answer, (CRaP) for incorrect answer.

SCORE:

Team A - Round 2

Team B, get ready to ask Team A these five questions. Every correct answer is worth one point. Get all five right and score a bonus 2 points.

1	A barnacle is a crusty bacterium that grows like moss underwater.	**FACT** CRaP
2	There is a point in Death Valley that measures 280 feet below sea level.	**FACT** CRaP
3	Johnny Cash did a cameo on *The Simpsons* as the voice of Maggie's pacifier.	**FACT** CRaP
4	One year on Pluto is the equivalent of 248 years on Earth.	**FACT** CRaP
5	Tadpoles are just like fish, except they don't have gills.	**FACT** CRaP

FACT for correct answer, **CRaP** for incorrect answer.

SCORE:

ANSWERS: 1) CRAP 2) FACT 3) CRAP 4) FACT 5) CRAP

Team B - Round 2

Team A, get ready to ask Team B these five questions. Every correct answer is worth one point. Get all five right and score a bonus 2 points.

1	Venereal disease gets its name from the Roman love goddess, Venus.	**FACT** CRaP
2	Miami is the capital of Florida.	**FACT** CRaP
3	7-Eleven stores across the country were transformed into *Simpsons*-inspired "Kwik-E-Marts" in 2007.	**FACT** CRaP
4	Wild turkeys can't fly, but they can run very fast.	**FACT** CRaP
5	The "legs" of a wine refers to the length of its bottleneck.	**FACT** CRaP

FACT for correct answer, **CRaP** for incorrect answer.

SCORE:

Team A - Rush Hour

Team B, get ready to call out the questions. Answer all questions correctly for 10 points, but get just one wrong and you score zilch.

1	Warren Harding served only two and a half years as president.	**FACT** CRaP
2	*Cantabile* refers to a kind of cheese-filled pasta.	**FACT** CRaP
3	Bugsy Siegel named the Flamingo casino in honor of his showgirl girlfriend's long legs.	**FACT** CRaP
4	The spire on the Notre Dame Cathedral in Strasbourg took 47 years to complete.	**FACT** CRaP
5	Florence Nightingale, the pioneer of modern nursing, was born in Florence, Italy.	**FACT** CRaP

FACT for correct answer, **CRaP** for incorrect answer.

SCORE:

Team B - Rush Hour

Team A, get ready to call out the questions. Answer all questions correctly for 10 points, but get just one wrong and you score zilch.

1	Toads are actually members of the reptile family, unlike frogs and salamanders.	**FACT** CRaP
2	Muhammed, who founded Islam, was orphaned early in his life, and raised by an uncle.	**FACT** CRaP
3	Bears are herbivores.	**FACT** CRaP
4	Picasso once painted a portrait of Virginia Woolf.	**FACT** CRaP
5	The country that purchases the most fireworks is Japan.	**FACT** CRaP

FACT for correct answer, **CRaP** for incorrect answer.

SCORE:

Game Thirteen - Total

There are only two answers in this game and only two places for your name!

Team A
Round 1 (+ bonus points):
Round 2 (+ bonus points):
Rush Hour:
Total:

Team B
Round 1 (+ bonus points):
Round 2 (+ bonus points):
Rush Hour:
Total:

See pages 174 and 175 and put your name where it belongs.

Game Fourteen

Another game full of fascinating facts,
with some Crap thrown in for fun.

Team A - Round 1

Team B, get ready to ask Team A these five questions. Every correct answer is worth one point. Get all five right and score a bonus 2 points.

1	Snakes don't have bones, just layers of muscles.	**FACT** CRaP
2	A castrato is a male singer who has been castrated in order to maintain his vocal range.	**FACT** CRaP
3	Soldiers in the Civil War received Hershey's Milk Chocolate Bars in their rations.	**FACT** CRaP
4	Space shuttles are capable of speeds up to 18,000mph.	**FACT** CRaP
5	Costa Rica is twice as large as Honduras.	**FACT** CRaP

(**FACT**) for correct answer, (CRaP) for incorrect answer.

SCORE:

Team B - Round 1

Team A, get ready to ask Team B these five questions. Every correct answer is worth one point. Get all five right and score a bonus 2 points.

1	Donald Trump once filed for business bankruptcy.	**FACT** CRaP
2	Tennis great Martina Navratilova is from Hungary.	**FACT** CRaP
3	Donald Trump and Rosie O'Donnell waged a very public battle in 2007.	**FACT** CRaP
4	In the Miss America pageant, the interview portion counts for 50% of the contestant's overall score.	**FACT** CRaP
5	The term speedo, though taken from a brand name, is now a "genericized trademark."	**FACT** CRaP

FACT for correct answer, **CRaP** for incorrect answer.

SCORE:

Team A - Round 2

Team B, get ready to ask Team A these five questions. Every correct answer is worth one point. Get all five right and score a bonus 2 points.

1	A colossal squid attacked a surfer off the coast of Santa Cruz in 2006.	**FACT** CRaP
2	Egypt was once ruled by a female pharaoh named Hatshepsut.	**FACT** CRaP
3	Eccentric designer Santino Rice won top honors in the fashion-based reality show *Project Runway*.	**FACT** CRaP
4	Bette Davis' tombstone reads, "She did it the hard way."	**FACT** CRaP
5	Alfred Hitchcock refused to be knighted in 1984.	**FACT** CRaP

(**FACT**) for correct answer, (**CRaP**) for incorrect answer.

SCORE:

Team B - Round 2

Team A, get ready to ask Team B these five questions. Every correct answer is worth one point. Get all five right and score a bonus 2 points.

1	Patriot is a city in Indiana.	**FACT** CRaP
2	If you come across a *forte* in a musical composition, you should play the part quietly.	**FACT** CRaP
3	Marvin Gaye was shot and killed by his own father.	**FACT** CRaP
4	In formal dining, the guest of honor should always be served after all of the other guests.	**FACT** CRaP
5	Julio Iglesias has sold more albums than Frank Sinatra.	**FACT** CRaP

(**FACT**) for correct answer, (CRaP) for incorrect answer.

SCORE:

Team A - Rush Hour

Team B, get ready to call out the questions. Answer all questions correctly for 10 points, but get just one wrong and you score zilch.

1	A "heady" wine is high in alcohol.	**FACT** CRaP
2	Vampire bats prey mostly on humans.	**FACT** CRaP
3	Only two countries border three oceans.	**FACT** CRaP
4	Chloe Sevigny won an Oscar for her role in *Boys Don't Cry*.	**FACT** CRaP
5	On *Twin Peaks*, Laura Palmer was killed by her father.	**FACT** CRaP

(**FACT**) for correct answer, (CRaP) for incorrect answer.

SCORE:

Team B - Rush Hour

Team A, get ready to call out the questions. Answer all questions correctly for 10 points, but get just one wrong and you score zilch.

1	Marlon Brando was a huge inspiration for actor Montgomery Clift.	**FACT** CRaP
2	The majority of Miami-Dade County, Florida's population is composed of foreign-born citizens.	**FACT** CRaP
3	Maybelline was the first cosmetics manufacturer to market non-theatrical makeup.	**FACT** CRaP
4	Papyrus is a paper made from a plant that grows along the Nile.	**FACT** CRaP
5	Al Gore's film, *An Inconvenient Truth*, was an expose of campaign finance scandals.	**FACT** CRaP

FACT for correct answer, **CRaP** for incorrect answer.

SCORE:

Game Fourteen - Total

Success is determined only by your ability to pick Fact from Crap.
It's time to add up your scores.

Team A	Team B
Round 1 (+ bonus points):	Round 1 (+ bonus points):
Round 2 (+ bonus points):	Round 2 (+ bonus points):
Rush Hour:	Rush Hour:
Total:	Total:

The Hall of Fame or Shame awaits you on pages 174 and 175.

Game Fifteen

If you keep on confusing facts with crap,
perhaps you should enter politics.

Team A - Round 1

Team B, get ready to ask Team A these five questions. Every correct answer is worth one point. Get all five right and score a bonus 2 points.

1	George Clinton produced the Red Hot Chili Pepper's album, *Freaky Style*.	**FACT** CRaP
2	The term *value* in drawing refers to the cost of the pencils.	**FACT** CRaP
3	Elian Gonzales was the name of the young Cuban boy who sparked a huge immigration controversy in 2000.	**FACT** CRaP
4	The show *MASH* was actually a spin-off of a medical sitcom starring Alan Alda.	**FACT** CRaP
5	Pennsylvania is the *Keystone State*.	**FACT** CRaP

(FACT) for correct answer, (CRaP) for incorrect answer.

SCORE:

Team B - Round 1

Team A, get ready to ask Team B these five questions. Every correct answer is worth one point. Get all five right and score a bonus 2 points.

1	Saddam Hussein was born into the wealthiest family in Baghdad.	**FACT** CRaP
2	Nike helped design "Koran-friendly" sportswear for Muslim women.	**FACT** CRaP
3	The word "ain't" was inducted into the Webster's dictionary in 2007.	**FACT** CRaP
4	Mercury lost its planet status in 2006, when it was downgraded to a dwarf planet instead.	**FACT** CRaP
5	Michael Jackson convinced his family members to become Jehovah's Witnesses.	**FACT** CRaP

FACT for correct answer, **CRaP** for incorrect answer.

SCORE:

Team A - Round 2

Team B, get ready to ask Team A these five questions. Every correct answer is worth one point. Get all five right and score a bonus 2 points.

1	Bette Davis and Jack Kerouac were born in the same Massachusetts town.	**FACT** CRaP
2	Bikinis date back to the era immediately following the second world war, when the soldiers returned.	**FACT** CRaP
3	Before becoming the Fonz, Henry Winkler played the role of a toothpaste tube.	**FACT** CRaP
4	Tara Conner had her Miss USA title revoked when she tested positive for drugs and alcohol.	**FACT** CRaP
5	Archaeologists claimed to find the remnants of Noah's ark lodged in Iran's Mount Suleiman.	**FACT** CRaP

(FACT) for correct answer, (CRaP) for incorrect answer.

SCORE:

ANSWERS: 1) FACT 2) CRAP 3) FACT 4) CRAP 5) FACT

Team B - Round 2

Team A, get ready to ask Team B these five questions. Every correct answer is worth one point. Get all five right and score a bonus 2 points.

1	Attila the Hun was born in Lithuania.	**FACT** CRaP
2	Al Gore won an Oscar for his movie, *An Inconvenient Truth*.	**FACT** CRaP
3	The primary colors are blue, orange and red.	**FACT** CRaP
4	A sea urchin possesses adhesive tube feet enabling it to move freely.	**FACT** CRaP
5	The top hospitality awards in the UK are called the *Cateys*.	**FACT** CRaP

(**FACT**) for correct answer, (**CRaP**) for incorrect answer.

SCORE:

Team A - Rush Hour

Team B, get ready to call out the questions. Answer all questions correctly for 10 points, but get just one wrong and you score zilch.

1	Wine connoisseurs describe a light, herbaceous wine as 'flinty.'	**FACT** CRaP
2	The original *3 Musketeers* bar featured one-part strawberry flavoring.	**FACT** CRaP
3	A John Dory is a rare cut of beef, often quite pricey.	**FACT** CRaP
4	463,000 immigrants became naturalized U.S. citizens in 2003.	**FACT** CRaP
5	Hawaii became the 50th state on December 17, 1944.	**FACT** CRaP

(FACT) for correct answer, (CRaP) for incorrect answer.

SCORE:

Team B - Rush Hour

Team A, get ready to call out the questions. Answer all questions correctly for 10 points, but get just one wrong and you score zilch.

1	The last person to be executed in the Tower of London was a German Spy named Josef Jakobs.	**FACT** CRaP
2	After the Civil War, General Lee made a bid for the presidency.	**FACT** CRaP
3	Crocodile dung was used as an Egyptian contraceptive until the early 20th century.	**FACT** CRaP
4	Venus spins in the opposite direction of all the other planets.	**FACT** CRaP
5	*The Mariana Trench* is the deepest spot in the Pacific ocean, at nearly 36,000 feet.	**FACT** CRaP

FACT for correct answer, CRaP for incorrect answer.

SCORE:

Game Fifteen - Total

FACT: It's not that difficult - there are only two answers to choose from!

Team A	Team B
Round 1 (+ bonus points):	Round 1 (+ bonus points):
Round 2 (+ bonus points):	Round 2 (+ bonus points):
Rush Hour:	Rush Hour:
Total:	Total:

So how did you score? Permanently inscribe your names where they belong.
Is it the Hall of Fame, or the sorry Hall of Shame?

Game Sixteen

Can you pick Fact from Crap?
Lift your game, or it's Shame not Fame.

Team A - Round 1

Team B, get ready to ask Team A these five questions. Every correct answer is worth one point. Get all five right and score a bonus 2 points.

1	The first person to have a star on the Hollywood Walk of Fame was Cole Porter.	**FACT** CRaP
2	The US suspended the death penalty in the '70s, only to reinstate it shortly thereafter.	**FACT** CRaP
3	California was the first state to use the gas chamber for executions.	**FACT** CRaP
4	Nazi SS troops had their blood type tattooed in their armpits.	**FACT** CRaP
5	Hundreds of Vegas hospital workers were suspended in a 2005 scandal for making bets on patient outcomes.	**FACT** CRaP

FACT for correct answer, CRaP for incorrect answer.

SCORE:

Team B - Round 1

Team A, get ready to ask Team B these five questions. Every correct answer is worth one point. Get all five right and score a bonus 2 points.

1	The first person to descend Niagara Falls in a barrel was a woman.	**FACT** CRaP
2	Lake Champlain was added to the Great Lakes in 2006.	**FACT** CRaP
3	Parkinson's disease attacks the central nervous system.	**FACT** CRaP
4	Stevie Wonder's blindness was actually caused by a birth defect.	**FACT** CRaP
5	*BAFTA* refers to an annual British entertainment awards show.	**FACT** CRaP

FACT for correct answer, **CRaP** for incorrect answer.

SCORE:

Team A - Round 2

Team B, get ready to ask Team A these five questions. Every correct answer is worth one point. Get all five right and score a bonus 2 points.

1	Ozzy Osbourne suffers from severe epilepsy as a result of his extended drug use.	**FACT** CRaP
2	Rumor has it Bruce Lee was poisoned for giving away too many martial arts secrets.	**FACT** CRaP
3	In drawing, "negative" space refers to that which is outside of the canvas itself.	**FACT** CRaP
4	The popular culinary dish *paella* was invented in Valencia, Spain and didn't initially feature seafood.	**FACT** CRaP
5	According to proper etiquette, wine is always poured from the left.	**FACT** CRaP

(FACT) for correct answer, (CRaP) for incorrect answer.

SCORE:

ANSWERS: 1) CRAP 2) FACT 3) CRAP 4) FACT 5) CRAP

Team B - Round 2

Team A, get ready to ask Team B these five questions. Every correct answer is worth one point. Get all five right and score a bonus 2 points.

1	No nation owns Antarctica.	**FACT** CRaP
2	Zebras share several genetic codes with skunks.	**FACT** CRaP
3	Pittsburgh Steelers' Ben Roethlisberger was in a nearly fatal motorcycle crash in 2006.	**FACT** CRaP
4	Penguins are actually marsupials.	**FACT** CRaP
5	Beyonce wore a padlocked dress to the 2007 BET awards.	**FACT** CRaP

FACT for correct answer, CRaP for incorrect answer.

SCORE:

ANSWERS: 1) FACT 2) CRaP 3) FACT 4) CRaP 5) FACT

Team A - Rush Hour

Team B, get ready to call out the questions. Answer all questions correctly for 10 points, but get just one wrong and you score zilch.

1	The Suez Canal connects the Northeast to the fertile areas along the Great Plains.	**FACT** CRaP
2	Jennifer Hudson was the first *American Idol* contestant to go on to win an Oscar.	**FACT** CRaP
3	In an executive kitchen, the *sous chef* is primarily responsible for pastries and cakes.	**FACT** CRaP
4	There is no talent section in the Miss USA pageant.	**FACT** CRaP
5	Hilary Clinton spoofed the opening scene of *The Sopranos* finale early in her '08 presidential run.	**FACT** CRaP

FACT for correct answer, CRaP for incorrect answer.

SCORE:

ANSWERS: 1) CRAP 2) FACT 3) CRAP 4) FACT 5) CRAP

Team B - Rush Hour

Team A, get ready to call out the questions. Answer all questions correctly for 10 points, but get just one wrong and you score zilch.

1	Angelina Jolie's baby Shiloh Nouvel was born in Namibia.	**FACT** CRaP
2	*Succotash* is a dish made from lima beans and corn.	**FACT** CRaP
3	In poker, a *dead man's hand* is aces and fours.	**FACT** CRaP
4	Max Factor started his cosmetics career as a wig maker.	**FACT** CRaP
5	The University of Chicago hosts one of the largest known scavenger hunts in the country.	**FACT** CRaP

(**FACT**) for correct answer, (CRaP) for incorrect answer.

SCORE:

Game Sixteen - Total

Who will be included into the Hall of Fame or Shame?
Add up all rounds to find out this game's winner.

Team A
Round 1 (+ bonus points):
Round 2 (+ bonus points):
Rush Hour:
Total:

Team B
Round 1 (+ bonus points):
Round 2 (+ bonus points):
Rush Hour:
Total:

Put yourself into the Hall of Fame or Hall of Shame on pages 174 and 175.

Game Seventeen

Fact: Some days you win and some days you're just Crap.

Team A - Round 1

Team B, get ready to ask Team A these five questions. Every correct answer is worth one point. Get all five right and score a bonus 2 points.

1	Zippo lighters are the world's most collected item.	**FACT** CRaP
2	Bras are referred to as *Y-fronts* in Britain.	**FACT** CRaP
3	Michigan was the first US state to abolish the death penalty.	**FACT** CRaP
4	Evander Holyfield was the youngest man to win a heavyweight title belt.	**FACT** CRaP
5	Green Day won two Nick Kids' Choice Awards in 2006.	**FACT** CRaP

(FACT) for correct answer, (CRaP) for incorrect answer.

SCORE:

ANSWERS: 1) CRAP 2) CRAP 3) FACT 4) CRAP 5) FACT

Team B - Round 1

Team A, get ready to ask Team B these five questions. Every correct answer is worth one point. Get all five right and score a bonus 2 points.

1	Paul McCartney wrote *Hey Jude* as a gift to Julian Lennon after John Lennon was killed.	**FACT** CRaP
2	*MASH*, the TV show, lasted eight years longer than the war it was based upon.	**FACT** CRaP
3	Ernest Hemingway once worked as a rodeo clown.	**FACT** CRaP
4	Flying squirrels don't really fly.	**FACT** CRaP
5	*Scrapple* is a uniquely American dish, featuring a gelatinous mass of varied piggy parts.	**FACT** CRaP

(FACT) for correct answer, (CRaP) for incorrect answer.

SCORE:

ANSWERS: 1) CRaP 2) FACT 3) CRaP 4) FACT 5) FACT

Team A - Round 2

Team B, get ready to ask Team A these five questions. Every correct answer is worth one point. Get all five right and score a bonus 2 points.

1	The monarch's transformation from caterpillar to butterfly takes about six months.	**FACT** CRaP
2	Hank Williams III, son of Hank Williams Jr., sometimes goes simply by 'III.'	**FACT** CRaP
3	Bo Jackson is the only athlete to have played in both a Super Bowl and a World Series.	**FACT** CRaP
4	Released in 2007, Apple's *iPhone* features 200 technology-related patents.	**FACT** CRaP
5	A Miss American pageant contestant once chose suitcase packing as her special talent.	**FACT** CRaP

(**FACT**) for correct answer, (CRaP) for incorrect answer.

SCORE:

Team B - Round 2

Team A, get ready to ask Team B these five questions. Every correct answer is worth one point. Get all five right and score a bonus 2 points.

1	Singapore carried out the most death penalty executions in 2006.	**FACT** CRaP
2	Actress Vivien Leigh smoked four packs a day during the filming of *Gone with the Wind*.	**FACT** CRaP
3	Alfred Hitchcock insisted that all of his actors improvise a majority of their scenes.	**FACT** CRaP
4	Benjamin Franklin wanted to replace the Bald Eagle with the Wild Turkey, as America's national bird.	**FACT** CRaP
5	*The Sopranos* ended their series run with a song by Foreigner in the final scene.	**FACT** CRaP

FACT for correct answer, **CRaP** for incorrect answer.

SCORE:

Team A - Rush Hour

Team B, get ready to call out the questions. Answer all questions correctly for 10 points, but get just one wrong and you score zilch.

1	Hungarians are known to fry up pig's blood with their scrambled eggs.	**FACT** CRaP
2	A death row inmate invented the electric chair.	**FACT** CRaP
3	Artist Raymond Pettibon is the brother of Black Flag founder Greg Ginn.	**FACT** CRaP
4	Baseball great Ty Cobb is known as the *Sultan of Swat*.	**FACT** CRaP
5	Each year, the swallows return to San Juan Capistrano, in southern California.	**FACT** CRaP

(FACT) for correct answer, (CRaP) for incorrect answer.

SCORE:

ANSWERS: 1) FACT 2) CRAP 3) FACT 4) CRAP 5) FACT

Team B - Rush Hour

Team A, get ready to call out the questions. Answer all questions correctly for 10 points, but get just one wrong and you score zilch.

1	Pinot Noir is one of the easiest grape varietals to grow.	**FACT** CRaP
2	The Swedish word *smorgasbord* literally translates as "sandwich table."	**FACT** CRaP
3	Charles de Gaulle was most famous for pioneering airplane technology.	**FACT** CRaP
4	*Hauso, llanero, gaucho* and *paniolo* all refer to cowboys from various geographical locations.	**FACT** CRaP
5	John F. Kennedy, a staunch Catholic, started the White House Easter Egg Roll.	**FACT** CRaP

FACT for correct answer, **CRaP** for incorrect answer.

SCORE:

Game Seventeen - Total

It's time to add up your scores, including all bonus points and see who's full of Crap.

Team A	Team B
Round 1 (+ bonus points):	Round 1 (+ bonus points):
Round 2 (+ bonus points):	Round 2 (+ bonus points):
Rush Hour:	Rush Hour:
Total:	Total:

The Hall of Fame or Shame awaits your scores on pages 174 and 175.

Game Eighteen

Here are another thirty tricky trivia tid-bits, just to tease you some more.

Team A - Round 1

Team B, get ready to ask Team A these five questions. Every correct answer is worth one point. Get all five right and score a bonus 2 points.

1	*Sockeye, humpback, Chinook* and chum are all types of salmon.	**FACT** CRaP
2	Florida is known as the *Golden State*.	**FACT** CRaP
3	Morocco was the first African country to join the African Union.	**FACT** CRaP
4	Michael Jordan holds the record for most *Sports Illustrated* covers - at 49.	**FACT** CRaP
5	Drivers should stop immediately, wherever they are, when they hear emergency sirens.	**FACT** CRaP

(FACT) for correct answer, (CRaP) for incorrect answer.

SCORE:

Team B - Round 1

Team A, get ready to ask Team B these five questions. Every correct answer is worth one point. Get all five right and score a bonus 2 points.

1	Vincent van Gogh worked as a schoolteacher and a missionary worker.	**FACT** CRaP
2	Singer Nora Jones is the daughter of Eric Clapton.	**FACT** CRaP
3	*Hearts and arrows* refers to a specific style of diamond cut.	**FACT** CRaP
4	FEMA, the U.S.' emergency management agency, was dissolved after Hurricane Katrina.	**FACT** CRaP
5	Spider-Man creator Stan Lee once attended a seminary with hopes of becoming a priest.	**FACT** CRaP

(**FACT**) for correct answer, (CRaP) for incorrect answer.

SCORE:

Team A - Round 2

Team B, get ready to ask Team A these five questions. Every correct answer is worth one point. Get all five right and score a bonus 2 points.

1	A mule is the offspring of a donkey and a horse.	**FACT** CRaP
2	A *fractal* is any unsymmetrical image or shape.	**FACT** CRaP
3	Horse sashimi is served up regularly in Japanese sushi joints.	**FACT** CRaP
4	The famous "running of the bulls" occurs in Barcelona, Spain.	**FACT** CRaP
5	Leonardo is the leader of the *Teenage Mutant Ninja Turtles*.	**FACT** CRaP

(FACT) for correct answer, (CRaP) for incorrect answer.

SCORE:

Team B - Round 2

Team A, get ready to ask Team B these five questions. Every correct answer is worth one point. Get all five right and score a bonus 2 points.

1	The first commercial whoopee cushion was invented by a British royal.	**FACT** CRaP
2	An *adadromous* fish does its breeding upstream, in fresh water.	**FACT** CRaP
3	Starsky and Hutch drove a red Camaro.	**FACT** CRaP
4	Snoopy's brother lives in Needles, California.	**FACT** CRaP
5	A *canolli* is used as a lethal weapon in the *Godfather* series.	**FACT** CRaP

(**FACT**) for correct answer, (**CRaP**) for incorrect answer.

SCORE:

ANSWERS: 1) CRAP 2) FACT 3) CRAP 4) FACT 5) FACT

Team A - Rush Hour

Team B, get ready to call out the questions. Answer all questions correctly for 10 points, but get just one wrong and you score zilch.

1	Wilco, The Shins and the Flaming Lips are all bands that have appeared on the kids' cartoon, *SpongeBob Squarepants*.	**FACT** CRaP
2	The Live Earth concert of 2007 was designed to raise money for AIDS research.	**FACT** CRaP
3	Sweden has found a way to fuel its public transportation system using smuggled booze.	**FACT** CRaP
4	Jeff Koons created his *Michael Jackson and Bubbles* sculpture as part of his "Banality" series.	**FACT** CRaP
5	Frogs are found only in the U.S.	**FACT** CRaP

(**FACT**) for correct answer, (CRaP) for incorrect answer.

SCORE:

Team B - Rush Hour

Team A, get ready to call out the questions. Answer all questions correctly for 10 points, but get just one wrong and you score zilch.

1	The *cochlea* is the thin bone attached to the Achilles tendon.	**FACT** CRaP
2	Lightning is three times hotter than the sun.	**FACT** CRaP
3	An *anemometer* measures mercury levels in fish.	**FACT** CRaP
4	A *dactyl* is a poetic term for a metrical foot containing three syllables.	**FACT** CRaP
5	The *guapacha* is a type of sweet Mexican melon.	**FACT** CRaP

(FACT) for correct answer, (CRaP) for incorrect answer.

SCORE:

Game Eighteen - Total

There are only two answers in this game and only two places for your name!

Team A	Team B
Round 1 (+ bonus points):	Round 1 (+ bonus points):
Round 2 (+ bonus points):	Round 2 (+ bonus points):
Rush Hour:	Rush Hour:
Total:	Total:

See pages 174 and 175 and put your name where it belongs.

Game Nineteen

How come the Crap answers sound so right?
Or are you smarter than that?

Team A - Round 1

Team B, get ready to ask Team A these five questions. Every correct answer is worth one point. Get all five right and score a bonus 2 points.

1	*Otoplasty* refers to surgery of the ear.	**FACT** CRaP
2	The *Thrilla in Manila* refers to a huge roller coaster in the Philippines.	**FACT** CRaP
3	A Hollywood movie version of the board game Clue was released in 1985.	**FACT** CRaP
4	*Thigmotaxis* is a skin disease resulting in clusters of itchy bumps.	**FACT** CRaP
5	The fine hair that covers and protects a fetus is called *lanugo*.	**FACT** CRaP

(FACT) for correct answer, (CRaP) for incorrect answer.

SCORE:

Team B - Round 1

Team A, get ready to ask Team B these five questions. Every correct answer is worth one point. Get all five right and score a bonus 2 points.

1	An undersea earthquake in the Indian Ocean caused the devastating 2004 tsunami.	**FACT** CRaP
2	The Prado is a famous bull-fighting ring in Spain.	**FACT** CRaP
3	Amity Island, the fictional coastal town in the Jaws movies, was filmed at Martha's Vineyard.	**FACT** CRaP
4	Ladybird was the name of Will Roger's dog.	**FACT** CRaP
5	Roger Ebert was the first person to win a Pulitzer Prize for film criticism.	**FACT** CRaP

(FACT) for correct answer, (CRaP) for incorrect answer.

SCORE:

Team A - Round 2

Team B, get ready to ask Team A these five questions. Every correct answer is worth one point. Get all five right and score a bonus 2 points.

1	The largest concentration of koalas is located in Tasmania and Western Australia.	**FACT** CRaP
2	*Broca's Aphasia* affects the part of the brain that forms words.	**FACT** CRaP
3	A Japanese *senryu* refers to a specific type of metal-plated chopsticks.	**FACT** CRaP
4	WWF wrestler Michael Depoli (aka "Roadkill") dresses in Amish garb and claims to be from Lancaster, Pennsylvania.	**FACT** CRaP
5	The viola is similar to the violin, but its sound is thinner and higher pitched.	**FACT** CRaP

(**FACT**) for correct answer, (CRaP) for incorrect answer.

SCORE:

Team B - Round 2

Team A, get ready to ask Team B these five questions. Every correct answer is worth one point. Get all five right and score a bonus 2 points.

1	*Burgoo* is a slow-cooked stew particularly popular in Kentucky.	**FACT** CRaP
2	Martok was the name of ALF's home planet on the '80s sitcom.	**FACT** CRaP
3	*Yuba* is a high protein soy by-product created by skimming the film off of soy milk.	**FACT** CRaP
4	Bullwinkle's sidekick is a chipmunk named Rocky.	**FACT** CRaP
5	Barbie's high fashion wardrobe features couture items by Versace, Dolce & Gabana, Gucci and Vera Wang.	**FACT** CRaP

FACT for correct answer, CRaP for incorrect answer.

SCORE:

Team A - Rush Hour

Team B, get ready to call out the questions. Answer all questions correctly for 10 points, but get just one wrong and you score zilch.

1	The triathlon is an athletic competition consisting of swimming, running and hurdles.	**FACT** CRaP
2	*Pisco* is a liquor made from grapes, popular in Peru and Chile.	**FACT** CRaP
3	Charmin was the first toilet paper manufacturer to wrap the sheets around a roll.	**FACT** CRaP
4	A *mandolin* is both a musical instrument and a cooking utensil.	**FACT** CRaP
5	Robin Williams first professional gig was playing Mork on *Mork and Mindy*.	**FACT** CRaP

FACT for correct answer, **CRaP** for incorrect answer.

SCORE:

ANSWERS: 1) CRAP 2) FACT 3) CRAP 4) FACT 5) CRAP

Team B - Rush Hour

Team A, get ready to call out the questions. Answer all questions correctly for 10 points, but get just one wrong and you score zilch.

1	*Grunge* music is associated mostly with Generation X.	**FACT** CRaP
2	The word *brulee* is French, meaning sweet milk.	**FACT** CRaP
3	The *Borscht Belt* is the nickname given to a resort area in upstate New York's Catskills frequented by Jewish vacationers.	**FACT** CRaP
4	A furlong is equal to eight miles.	**FACT** CRaP
5	The *Lazarus Phenomenon* refers to a syndrome in which the sufferer believes he is Jesus Christ.	**FACT** CRaP

(**FACT**) for correct answer, (CRaP) for incorrect answer.

SCORE:

Game Nineteen - Total

Success is determined only by your ability to pick Fact from Crap. It's time to add up your scores.

Team A	Team B
Round 1 (+ bonus points):	Round 1 (+ bonus points):
Round 2 (+ bonus points):	Round 2 (+ bonus points):
Rush Hour:	Rush Hour:
Total:	Total:

The Hall of Fame or Shame awaits you on pages 174 and 175.

Game Twenty

It's your last chance to sort the fact from the crap and get your name and score into the Hall of Fame.

Team A - Round 1

Team B, get ready to ask Team A these five questions. Every correct answer is worth one point. Get all five right and score a bonus 2 points.

1	Popular in the Basque country, the *kalimotxo* is a beverage blending red wine and Coco-cola.	**FACT** CRaP
2	Hello Kitty was originally designed as a rabbit named Hoppy Bunny.	**FACT** CRaP
3	Comedian Lenny Bruce received a posthumous pardon for an indecency conviction in the '60s.	**FACT** CRaP
4	Tuberculosis is an infectious disease caused by an overdose of the bacteria in tubers.	**FACT** CRaP
5	In 1873, reports indicate that a rain of frogs fell from the sky in Kansas City, Missouri.	**FACT** CRaP

FACT for correct answer, **CRaP** for incorrect answer.

SCORE:

ANSWERS: 1) FACT 2) CRAP 3) FACT 4) CRAP 5) FACT

Team B - Round 1

Team A, get ready to ask Team B these five questions. Every correct answer is worth one point. Get all five right and score a bonus 2 points.

1	A lepidopterist studies patterns of spots on spotted animals.	**FACT** CRaP
2	Human milk banks store donated breast milk for use by mothers who are unable to produce their own.	**FACT** CRaP
3	The Pink Pistols are an underground lesbian gang based in Washington, D.C.	**FACT** CRaP
4	*Pavo*, or the peacock, is a constellation best spotted in the September sky.	**FACT** CRaP
5	An extraordinarily high number of secular examples of stigmata were reported near the end of the 21st century.	**FACT** CRaP

FACT for correct answer, **CRaP** for incorrect answer.

SCORE:

Team A - Round 2

Team B, get ready to ask Team A these five questions. Every correct answer is worth one point. Get all five right and score a bonus 2 points.

1	In sewing terms, to *baste* is to use large stitches to join fabrics in a temporary fashion.	**FACT** CRaP
2	Maui's Haleakala volcano has experienced over a dozen major eruptions in the last decade.	**FACT** CRaP
3	Model Kathy Ireland graced the cover of the best-selling *Sports Illustrated Swimsuit* Issue.	**FACT** CRaP
4	The family-friendly 1970s TV show *Grizzly Adams* was first released as a horror movie in the late '60s.	**FACT** CRaP
5	Hockey star Wayne Gretzky is known to fans as "the Great One."	**FACT** CRaP

(FACT) for correct answer, (CRaP) for incorrect answer.

SCORE:

ANSWERS: 1) FACT 2) CRAP 3) FACT 4) CRAP 5) FACT

Team B - Round 2

Team A, get ready to ask Team B these five questions. Every correct answer is worth one point. Get all five right and score a bonus 2 points.

1	*Super Freak* singer Rick James was a medaled naval soldier prior to his singing career.	**FACT** CRaP
2	After conquering neighboring China, Mongol leader Genghis Kahn allowed the Chinese to maintain their own customs and religion.	**FACT** CRaP
3	Jennifer Lopez claims all three of her Doberman Pinschers are vegetarian.	**FACT** CRaP
4	The canary sings a twittering song similar to that of the goldfinch.	**FACT** CRaP
5	Prior to entering the circus business, P.T. Barnum was a doctor who specialized in deformities.	**FACT** CRaP

FACT for correct answer, **CRaP** for incorrect answer.

SCORE:

Team A - Rush Hour

Team B, get ready to call out the questions. Answer all questions correctly for 10 points, but get just one wrong and you score zilch.

1	Thomas Jefferson is on the two-dollar bill.	**FACT** CRaP
2	The Giant Panda isn't classified as a bear at all - it belongs to the raccoon family!	**FACT** CRaP
3	Minnesota, as the head of the "Corn Belt," produces 50% of all corn in the U.S.	**FACT** CRaP
4	Butter was considered so sacred in Ancient Egypt that King Tut's mummified body was slathered in it.	**FACT** CRaP
5	The term *hot dog* came from a cartoonist who accused Coney Island of using dog meat in their wieners.	**FACT** CRaP

(**FACT**) for correct answer, (CRaP) for incorrect answer.

SCORE:

Team B - Rush Hour

Team A, get ready to call out the questions. Answer all questions correctly for 10 points, but get just one wrong and you score zilch.

1	Salsa dancing has been banned in Cuba since Fidel Castro's 1959 revolution.	**FACT** CRaP
2	The band Bright Eyes performed with Bruce Springsteen and R.E.M. as part of the '04 MoveOn political tour.	**FACT** CRaP
3	The *Sloppy Joe* is named after Joe DiMaggio, a notoriously messy eater.	**FACT** CRaP
4	The branch-like arms of the snowflake are called *dendrites*.	**FACT** CRaP
5	*Amuse buche* is a French term for a variety of cream-filled desserts.	**FACT** CRaP

FACT for correct answer, **CRaP** for incorrect answer.

SCORE:

Game Twenty - Total

FACT: It's not that difficult – there are only two answers to choose from!

Team A	Team B
Round 1 (+ bonus points):	Round 1 (+ bonus points):
Round 2 (+ bonus points):	Round 2 (+ bonus points):
Rush Hour:	Rush Hour:
Total:	Total:

So how did you score? Permanently inscribe your names where they belong. Is it the Hall of Fame, or the sorry Hall of Shame?

Notes

Notes

Notes

Notes

Notes

Notes

Notes

Hall of Fame

The Fact is, for your name and score to be entered here, you are either so much smarter than everyone else ... or, when it comes to playing by the rules and Keeping an honest score, you're actually full of Crap!

NAME:	SCORE:	NAME:	SCORE: